MYSTERY IN THE SKIES

Contents

UFOs — page 2

The Case of the UFO Pictures — page 16

Simon Cheshire

Story illustrated by
Ned Woodman

Heinemann

Find out about

- The different reports of UFOs from around the world

Tricky words

- saucers
- aliens
- spying
- hovered
- radio
- airfield
- terrified
- astronauts

Introduce these tricky words and help the reader when they come across them later!

Text starter

A UFO is an Unidentified Flying Object. UFOs come in many shapes. People have reported seeing strange lights, hearing strange noises and even seeing the bodies of dead aliens.

UFOS

UFOs in America

Lots of people all over the world say they have seen strange flying objects in the sky.

In 1947, there was a report of UFOs.

A pilot said they looked like shining discs.

So people called them flying saucers!

One month later, a UFO was reported to have crashed in a desert.
The army said it was a weather balloon that had crashed, but the people who lived nearby said they had seen a spaceship.
Some people even said they had seen the bodies of dead aliens!

Does this weather balloon look like a UFO?

CRASH SITE

URS: 623-8104

useum - 114 N. Main - Roswell

Why would the army say it was a weather balloon if it was not?

Why would people say they had seen a spaceship or dead aliens if they had not?

Who was right – the army or the people?

UFOs in Europe

In 1980, hundreds of people reported seeing a strange light in the sky over London. One man even took a video of it! At first the light hovered, then it shot across the sky. It stopped again before zooming off at a very high speed! Had all these people seen a UFO?

In 1989, a bright light was seen in the sky above an army camp in Hungary.

The soldiers said they heard strange noises and they saw three UFOs. The UFOs hovered in the sky and then zoomed off. One month later, they saw the UFOs again. Were there aliens in the UFOs, spying on the army?

UFOs in Australia

A pilot in a small plane reported on his radio that he could see a UFO.

"I can see a strange object in the sky. It isn't another plane. I don't know what it is. It's long and shiny and it's coming at me ..."

Those were the last words the people at the airfield heard, and they lost radio contact with the pilot.

The plane never landed at the airfield. Four years later, the plane was found at the bottom of the sea.

What had the pilot seen, and what happened to him?

UFOs in China

In 1990, two soldiers were driving a jeep. Suddenly, they saw a huge black disc hovering in the sky just above their jeep. The soldiers were terrified. They thought it was an alien spaceship. They tried to speed away but the strange black disc stayed hovering above them.

The soldiers stopped their jeep but the strange disc stopped too!

The terrified soldiers jumped out of the jeep. The black disc was hovering just above their heads. The soldiers thought it was going to attack them. Then, as quickly as it had arrived, the strange disc zoomed off. Was something (or someone) trying to kidnap the soldiers?

UFOs in South America

In 1980, people reported seeing a UFO. Two jet fighter-planes were sent to attack it. They fired and fired at the UFO but their rockets did not damage it in any way. The fighter-planes chased the UFO but it suddenly vanished.

UFOs in Space

In 1969, when astronauts went to the Moon, they reported seeing a strange light in Space. They reported it to Mission Control but Mission Control could not explain it.

On other missions, astronauts have also reported seeing strange flying objects in Space. Could it be that aliens are trying to make contact with Earth?

Do you think these reports about UFOs are true? Are aliens sending UFOs to Earth? Do they want to attack us, or do they want to just make contact with us?

If you saw a UFO, what would you do?

Text Detective

- What do the letters UFO stand for?
- Would you be scared if you saw a UFO?

Word Detective

- Phonic Focus: Unstressed vowels
  Page 4: Which letters represent the unstressed vowel in 'weather'? (er)
- Page 8: Why does the last sentence end with dots?
- Page 9: Find a word made from two words.

Super Speller

Read these words:

these   also   four

Now try to spell them!

HA! HA! HA!

Q What did the alien-spotter have for dinner?

A An unidentified frying object.

In this story

 Harry

 Kate

 Josh

 Josh's mum

Tricky words

- interview
- radio
- photos
- digital
- aliens
- neighbours

Introduce these tricky words and help the reader when they come across them later!

Story starter

Harry and Kate are members of SCARY, a secret club that investigates spooky mysteries. One day, they heard that a boy called Josh had said he had taken photos of a UFO.

The Case of the UFO Pictures

"Josh is so lucky to have seen a UFO," said Harry.

"We need to speak to him and find out what really happened," said Kate.

When they got to Josh's house, he was doing an interview with the local radio.

Josh's mum showed Harry and Kate the photos of the UFO that Josh had taken. The photos showed a silver disc high up in the night sky. They could also make out the fence at the end of Josh's garden.

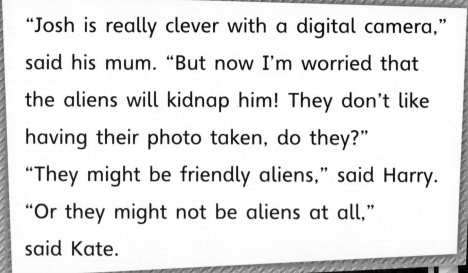

"Josh is really clever with a digital camera," said his mum. "But now I'm worried that the aliens will kidnap him! They don't like having their photo taken, do they?"

"They might be friendly aliens," said Harry.

"Or they might not be aliens at all," said Kate.

"Yes they *are* aliens!" said Josh as he ran into the room. "That's a real UFO, I saw it! You just wish you'd seen it yourself!"

"Yes," said Harry. "I'd love to see a UFO."

"So would I," said Kate, "if I could be sure it was real. When did you take these photos?"

"Last Saturday," said Josh. "They've been in all the papers, and shown on TV. I'm famous now!"

Kate looked at the photos carefully.
"The UFO must have been about
thirty metres long," she said.
"Yes," said Josh. "It was huge!"
"Can we borrow these photos?"
asked Harry.
"OK," said Josh.

Harry was very excited.

"These photos prove that the UFO was real!" he said.

"They seem to be proof," said Kate. "But I'm not so sure. We need to check. Let's talk to the neighbours."

They knocked on the door of every house in the street, then every house in the next street. Nobody had seen a UFO last Saturday. Kate was puzzled.

"But Josh said it was huge!" she said.

"Why didn't anyone else see it?"

"Well," said Harry, "maybe everyone was asleep or watching TV, or away for the weekend. Anyway, Josh took the photos of the UFO. That's all the proof we need."

Do you think the photo proves there was a UFO?

When Kate got home she looked at the photos again.

"Harry!" she called. "Come and have a look. Can you see that very thin line, running up from the top of the UFO and out of the photo?"

"Yes," said Harry. "It could be a scratch on the film."

"No, it can't be," said Kate. "Josh has a
digital camera. It doesn't use film.
I bet Josh took a photo of a model UFO
– that thin line is a wire, holding it up.
Then he took a photo of the sky, and
put the two photos together on
the computer!"

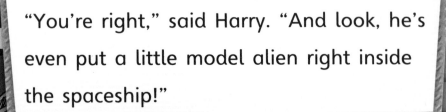

"You're right," said Harry. "And look, he's even put a little model alien right inside the spaceship!"

They went back to Josh's house.
"You didn't really see a UFO did you?" said Kate.
"No," said Josh. "I only wanted to be famous."

"You were clever with the photos,"
said Kate. "Except for the wire, and
the toy alien."

"What toy alien?" asked Josh.
He looked at the photos very carefully.
Suddenly he went very pale.

"I don't have any toy aliens,"
he said quietly.

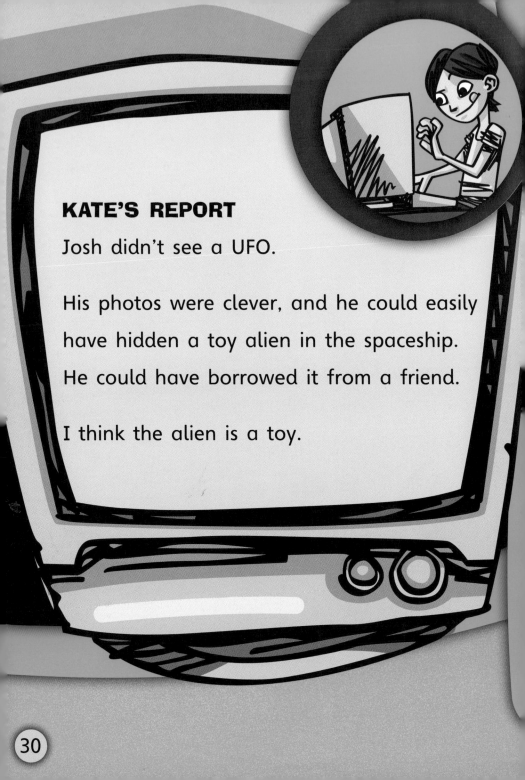

KATE'S REPORT

Josh didn't see a UFO.

His photos were clever, and he could easily have hidden a toy alien in the spaceship. He could have borrowed it from a friend.

I think the alien is a toy.

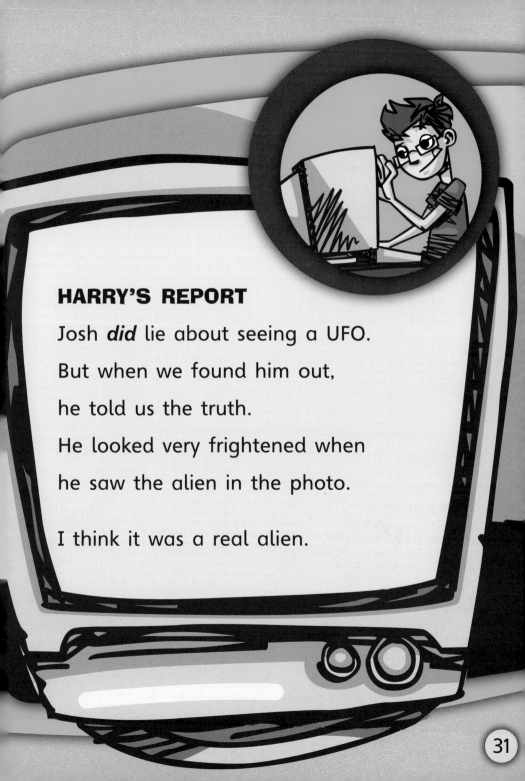

HARRY'S REPORT

Josh *did* lie about seeing a UFO.
But when we found him out,
he told us the truth.
He looked very frightened when
he saw the alien in the photo.

I think it was a real alien.

Quiz

Text Detective

- Why did Josh pretend he saw a UFO?
- What would you do to be famous?

Word Detective

- **Phonic Focus**: Unstressed vowels

  Page 21: Which letters represent the unstressed vowel in 'Saturday'? (ur)
- Page 21: Why does the word 'Saturday' start with a capital letter?
- Page 21: Which letter does the apostrophe replace in 'I'm'?

Super Speller

Read these words:

wanted   really   Saturday

Now try to spell them!

HA! HA! HA!

Q What did the alien find in the kitchen cupboard?

A A flying saucer.